FUCK THE SYSTEM

"George Metesky"

FIRST PUBLISHED, 1967.

FUCK THE SYSTEM WAS A YIPPIES GUIDE FOR THOSE WANT-ING TO LIVING OFF THE EXCESSES OF THE CAPITALIST SYSTEM IN NEW YORK CITY. COMPILED UNDER THE NAME GEORGE METESKY, THE "MAD BOMBER" WHO PLANTED BOMBS IN NEW YORK DURING THE 1940S AND 1950S,

THE GUIDE'S CONTENT PREFIGURED THE BETTER KNOWN AND MORE WIDELY DISSEMINATED *STEAL THIS BOOK* (1971).

Take what you want
Take what you need
There is plenty to go around
Everything is free.

George Metesky

Free

New York

YIPPIEEEEEEEEEEEEEEEEEEEEEEEEEEEEEEEEEEEEEEEEEEEEEEEEEEEEEEEEEEEE

TABLE OF CONTENTS

Free Food 4
Welfare 7
Free Clothes 8
Free Lawyers 8
Free Flowers 8
Free Furniture 9
Free Transportation 9
Free Phone Calls 10
Free Money 10
Free Gas 11
Free Land 12
Free Buffalo 12
Free Medical Help 12
Emergency Numbers 12
Free Drugs 13
Free Security 13
Free Birth Control Information 13
Free Information (General) 14
Free Rent 15
Free Beaches 16
Free College 16
Free Theatre 16
Free Movies 17
Free Music 18
Free Museums 18
Free Poetry 20
Free Swimming Pools 20
Free Pets 21
Draft Resistance 21
Free Cars 21
Clap Section 22
Cop Section 23
Dope Tips and Bad Trips 26
Communes 29

FREE VEGETABLES — Hunt's Point Market, Hunt's Point Avenue and 138th Street. Have to go by car or truck between 6-9 A.M. but well worth it. You can get enough vegetables to last your commune a week. Lettuce, squash, carrots, canteloupe, grapefruit, melons, even artichokes and mushrooms. Just tell them you want to feed some people free and it's yours, all crated and everything. Hunt's Point is the free people's heaven.

FREE MEAT AND POULTRY — The closest slaughterhouse area is in the far West Village, west of Hudson Street and south of 14th Street. Get a letter from Rev. Allen of St. Mark's on the Bowerie, Second Avenue and 10th Street, saying you need some meat for a church sponsored meal. If you want to be really professional, dress as a priest and go over and ask. Bring a car or truck. A freezer unit will save a good deal of running around. Don't give up on this one. Turning a guy onto the free idea will net you a week's supply of top quality meat. There is some law that if the meat touches the ground or floor they have to give it away. So if you know how to trip a meat truck, by all means . . .

FREE FRESH FISH — The Fish Market is located on Fulton Street and South Street under the East River Drive overpass. You have to get there between 6 - 9 A.M. but it is well worth it. The fishermen always have hundreds of pounds of fish that they have to throw away if they don't sell. Mackerel, halibut, cod, catfish, and more. You can have as much as you can cart away.

FREE BREAD AND ROLLS — Rapaports on Second Avenue between 5th and 6th Streets will give you all the free bread and rolls you can carry. You have to get there by 7:00 A.M. in order to get the stuff. It's a day old, but still very good. If you want them absolutely fresh, put them in an oven to which you have added a pan of water (to avoid drying them out), and warm them for a few minutes. Most bakeries will give you day old stuff if you give them a half way decent sob story.

★   ★   ★

A&P stores clean their vegetable bins every day at 9:00 A.M. They always throw out cartons of very good vegetables. Tell them you want to feed your rabbits. Also recommended is picking up food in a supermarket and eating it before you leave the store. This method is a lot safer than the customary shoplifting. In order to be prosecuted for shoplifting you have to leave the store with the goods. If you have eaten it, there is no evidence to be used against you.

FREE COOKING LESSONS — (Plus you get to eat the meal) are sponsored by the New York Department of Markets, 137 Centre Street. Thursday mornings. Call CA 6-5653 for more information.

Check the Yellow Pages for Catering Services. You can visit them on a Saturday, Sunday afternoon or Monday morning. They always have stuff left over. Invest 10c in one of the Jewish Dailies and check out the addresses of the local synagogues and their schedule of bar mitzvahs, weddings, and testimonial dinners. Show up at the back of the place about three hours after it is scheduled to start. There is always left-over food. Tell them you're a college student and want to bring some back for your fraternity brothers. Jews dig the college bullshit. If you want the food served to you out front you naturally have to disguise yourself to look straight. Remarks such as "I'm Marvin's brother" or — learning the bride's name from the paper — "Gee, Dorothy looks marvelous" are great. Lines like "Betty doesn't look pregnant" are frowned upon.

★ ★ ★

Large East Side bars are fantastically easy touches. The best time is 5:00 P.M. Take a half empty glass of booze from an empty table and use it as a prop. Just walk around sampling the hors d'oeuvres. Once you find your favorite, stick to it. You can soon become a regular. They won't mind your loading up on free food because they consider you one of the crowd. Little do they realize that you are a super freeloader. All Longchamps are good. Max's Kansas City at Park Avenue South and 16th Street doesn't even mind it if you freeload when you are hungry and an advantage here is that you can wear any kind of clothes. Max features fried chicken wings, swedish meatballs and ravioli.

★ ★ ★

THE INTERNATIONAL SOCIETY FOR KRISHNA CONSCIOUSNESS is located at 26 Second Avenue. Every morning at 7:00 A.M. a delicious cereal breakfast is served free along with chanting and dancing. Also 12 Noon more food and chanting and on Monday, Wednesday and Friday at 7:00 P.M. again food and chanting. Then it's all day Sunday in Central Park Sheepmeadow (generally) for still more chanting (sans food). Hari Krishna is the freest high going if you can get into it and dig cereal and, of course, more chanting.

FREE TEA AND COOKIES — In a very nice setting at the Tea Center, 16 East 56th Street. 10 - 11 A.M. and 2 - 4 P.M. Monday to Friday.

THE CATHOLIC WORKER — 181 Chrystie Street, will feed you any time but you have to pray as you do in the various Salvation Army stations. Heavy wino scenes. The heaviest wino scene is the **Men's Temporary Shelter** on 8 East 3rd Street. You can get free room and / or meals here if you are over 21 but it's worse than jail or Bellevue. It is a definite last resort only.

★ ★ ★

The freest meal of all is Tuesdays at 5:00 P.M. inside or in front of St. Mark's Church on the Bowerie, Second Avenue at 10th Street. A few yippie-diggers serve up a meal ranging from Lion Meat to Guppy Chowder to Canteloupe Salad. They are currently looking for a free truck to help them collect the food and free souls dedicated to extending the free food concept. The Motherfuckers also dish out free food on St. Mark's Place from time to time.

If you are really looking for class, pick up a copy of the **New York Times** and check the box in the back pages designating ocean cruises. On every departure there is a bon voyage party. Just walk on a few hours before sailing time and start swinging. Champagne, caviar, lobster salad, all as free as the open sea. If you get stoned enough and miss getting off you can also wiggle a free boat ride although you get sent back as soon as you hit the other side — but it's a free ocean cruise, even if it's in the brig.

★ ★ ★

You can get free food in varying quantities by going to the factories. Many also offer a free tour. However, the plants are generally located outside of Manhattan. If you can get a car, try a trip to Long Island City. There you will find the Gordon Baking Company at 42-25 21st Street, Pepsi-Cola at 4602 Fifth Avenue, Borden Company at 35-10 Steinway Street and Dannon Yogurt at 22-11 38th Avenue. All four places give out free samples and if you write or call in advance and say it is for a block party or church affair, they will give you a few cases.

★ ★ ★

FREE BOOZE — Jacob Ruppert Brewery at 1639 Third Avenue near 91st Street will give you a tour at 10:30 A.M. and 2:30 P.M. complete with free booze in their tap room.

★ ★ ★

The Sun is free. Hair is freee. Naked bodies are free. Smiles are free. Rain is free. Unfortunately there is no free air in New York. Con Edison's phone number is 679-6700.

WELFARE — If you live in lower Manhattan the welfare center for you is located on 11 West 13th Street, 989-1210. There is, of course, red tape involved and they don't dig longhairs. Be prepared to tell a good story as to why you cannot work, however your looks (which they cannot make you change) might be good enough reason. This is one place where sloppy clothes pay off. You have to be over 18 to get help. A caseworker will be assigned to you. Some will actually dig the whole scene and won't give you a hard time, others can be a real bitch. Getting on welfare can get you free rent, phone, utilities, and about $20.00 a week to live on. There are also various food stamp and medical programs you become eligible for. If you can stomach hassle, welfare is a must. The main office number is DI 4-8700 if you do not live in lower Manhattan.

★ ★ ★

FREE CLOTHES — Try ESSO, 341 East 10th Street or Tompkins Square Community Center on Avenue B and 9th Street. Also the streets are excellent places to pick up good clothes (see section on free furniture for best times to go hunting).

★ ★ ★

FREE LAWYERS — **Legal Aid Society**, 100 Centre Street, BE 3-0250 (criminal matters) and the **New York University Law Center Office**, 249 Sullivan Street, GR 3-1896 (civil matters). Also for specialized cases and information you can call the **National Lawyers Guild**, 5 Beekman Street, 227-1078 or the **New York Civil Liberties Union**, 156 Fifth Avenue, WA 9-6076. For the best help on the Lower East Side use **Mobilization for Youth Legal Services**, 320 East 3rd Street between Avenues C and D, OR 7-0400, ask for legal services. Open Tuesday to Friday, 9 A.M. to 6 P.M. and until 8 P.M. on Mondays. Some of the best lawyers in the city available here.

★ ★ ★

FREE FLOWERS — At about 9:30 A.M. each day you can bum free flowers in the Flower District on Sixth Avenue between 22nd and 23rd Streets. Once in a while you can find a potted tree that's been thrown out because it's slightly damaged.

FREE FURNITURE — By far the best place to get free furniture is on the street. Once a week in every district the sanitation department makes bulk pick-ups. The night before residents put out all kinds of stuff on the street. For the best selection try the West Village on Monday nights and the east Seventies on Tuesday nights. On Wedensday night there are fantastic pick-ups on 35th Street in back of Macy's. Move quickly though, the guards get pissed off easily; the truckers couldn't care less. This street method can furnish your whole pad. Beds, desks, bureaus, lamps, bookcases, chairs, and tables. It's all a matter of transportation. If you don't have access to a car or truck it is almost worth it to rent a station wagon on a weekday and make pick-ups. Alexander's Rent-a-Car is about the cheapest for in-city use. $5.95 and 10c a mile for a regular car. A station wagon is slightly more. Call AG 9-2200 for the branch near you.

Also consider demolition and construction sites as a good source for building materials to construct furniture. The large wooden cable spools make great tables. Cinderblocks, bricks and boards for bookcases. Doors for tables. Nail kegs for stools and chairs.

★ ★ ★

FREE BUS RIDES — Get on with a large denomination bill just as the bus is leaving.

FREE SUBWAY RIDES — Get a dark green card and flash it quickly as you go through the exit gate. Always test the swing bars in the turnstile before you put in the token. Someone during the day was sure to drop an extra token in and a free turn is just waiting for the first one to take advantage of it. By far the most creative method is the use of German fennigs, Danish ore or Mozambique 10 centavos pieces. These fit most turnstiles except the newest (carry a real token to use in case the freebee doesn't work). These foreign coins come four or five to a penny. Large amounts must be purchased outside New York City. Most dealers will not sell you large amounts since the

Transit Authority has been pressuring them. Try telling dealers you want them to make jewelry. Another interesting coin is the 5 aurar from Iceland. This is the same size as a quarter and will work in most vending machines. They sell for three or four to the penny. There are other coins that also work. Buy a bag of assorted foreign coins from a coin dealer and do a little measuring. You are sure to find some that fit the bill. Speaking of fitting the bill, we have heard that dollar bills can be duplicated on any Xerox machine (fronts done separately from backs and pasted together) and used in vending machines that give change for a dollar. This method has not been field tested.

★ ★ ★

The best form of free transportation is hitch-hiking. This is so novel in New York that it often works. Crosstown on 8th Street is good.

★ ★ ★

FREE PHONE CALLS — A number 14 brass washer with a small piece of scotch tape over one side of the hole will work in old style phones (also parking meters, laundromat dryers, soda and other vending machines). The credit card bit works on long distance calls. Code letter for 1968 is J, then a phone number and then a three digit district number. A district number, as well as the phone number, can be made up by using any three numbers from about 051 to 735. Example: J-573-2100-421 or J-637-3400-302. The phone number should end in 00 since most large corporations have numbers that end that way. The people that you call often get weird phone calls from the company but not much else. There are also legitimate credit card numbers available. One recent number belonged to Steve McQueen. A phone bill of $50,000 was racked up in one month. McQueen, of course, was not held responsible.

FREE MONEY — Panhandling nets some people up to Twenty

dollars a day. The best places are Third Avenue in the fifties and the Theater District off Times Square. Both best in the evening on weekends. Uptown guys with dates are the best touch especially if they are just leaving some guilt movie like "Guess Who's Coming to Dinner?" The professional panhandlers don't waste their time on the Lower East Side except on weekends when the tourists come out.

Devise a street theatre act or troupe. It can be anything from a funny dance to a five piece band or a poetry reading. People give a lot more dough and the whole atmosphere sings a little. SMILE! Panhandle at the rectories and nunneries on the side of every Catholic Church. Contrary to rumor the brother and sister freeloaders in black live very well and will always share something with a fellow panhandler.

Also see previous sections on the use of foreign coins.

★ ★ ★

FREE BOOKS AND RECORDS — If you have an address you can get all kinds of books and records from clubs on introductory offers. Since the cards you mail back are not signed there is no legal way you can be held responsible although you get all sorts of threatening mail, which, by the way, also comes free.

You can always use the Public Libraries. The main branch is on Fifth Avenue and 42nd Street. There are 168 branches all over the city. Call OX 5-4200 for information and a schedule of free events.

★ ★ ★

POEMS are free. Are you a poem or are you a prose???

★ ★ ★

FREE GAS — If you have a car and need some gas late at night you can get a gallon and then some by emptying the hoses from the pumps into your tank. There is always a fair amount of surplus gas left when the pumps are shut off.

FREE LAND — Write to "Green Revolution" c/o School of Living, Freeland, Maryland, for their free newspaper with news about rural land available in the United States and the progress of various rural communities. The best available free land is in Canada. You can get a free listing by writing to the Department of Land and Forests, Parliament Building, Quebec City, Canada. Also write to the Geographical Branch, Department of Mines and Technical Surveys, Parliament Buildings, Quebec City, Canada. Lynn Burrows, c/o Communications Group, 2630 Point Grey Rd., Vancouver 8, British Columbia, Canada, will give you the best information on setting up a community in Canada.

★ ★ ★

If you really want to live for free, get some friends together and seize a building at Columbia University. 116th Street and Broadway. The cops come free, as do blue ribbon committees with funny long names.

★ ★ ★

FREE BUFFALO — In order to keep the herds at a controllable level the government will give you a real, live buffalo if you can guarantee shipping expenses and adequate grazing area. Write to the Office of Information, Department of the Interior, Washington, D.C.

★ ★ ★

MEDICAID — Medicaid Center, 330 West Street, 594-3050. Medicaid is a very good deal if you can qualify and can stand a little red tape. According to the new law you have to be under 21 or over 65 years of age and have a low income ($2900 or less if you are single) to qualify. It takes about a month to process your application, but if you get a card you are entitled to free hospital and dental services, private physicians, drugs and many other medical advantages.

AMBULANCE SERVICE — Call 440-1234. You get a cop free of charge with this service. There is no way to get an ambulance without a cop in New York.

EMERGENCY DOCTOR — TR 9-1000.
EMERGENCY DENTIST — YU 8-6110.
NEARBY HOSPITALS —
Gouverneur Clinic, 9 Gouverneur Slip, 227-3000.
St. Vincent Hospital, 7th Ave. and West 11th St., 620-1234.
Bellevue Hospital, First Avenue and 27th Street, 679-5487.
On the above medical services you have to pay but you
can file the bill or send it to the National Digger Client
Center in Washington, D.C. They will pay it for you.

THE WASHINGTON HEIGHTS HEALTH CENTER — 168th Street
and Broadway, provides free chest X-rays as well as other
services. You can get a free smallpox vaccination here
at 10: A.M. weekdays if you're traveling abroad. Call WA
7-6300 for information.
See special section on clap in this booklet for information
on VD treatment.

★ ★ ★

FREE DRUGS — In the area along Central Park West in the
70's and 80's are located many doctor's offices. Daily
they throw out piles of drug samples. If you know what
you're looking for, search this area.

★ ★ ★

FREE SECURITY — For this trick you need some money to
begin with. Deposit it in a bank and return in a few weeks
telling them you lost your bank book. They give you a card
to fill out and sign and in a week you will receive another.
Now, withdraw your money, leaving you with your original
money and a bank book showing a balance. You can use
this as identification, to prevent vagrancy busts traveling,
as collateral for bail, or for opening a charge account at
a store.

★ ★ ★

FREE BIRTH CONTROL INFORMATION AND DEVICES — Clergy
Consultation Abortion, call 477-0034 and you will get a
recorded announcement giving you the names of clergy-
men who you can call and get birth control information,

including abortion contacts.

Parents Aid Society, 130 Main Street, Hempstead, Long Island, (516) 538-2626, provides by far the most complete birth control information. Pills are provided as well as diaphrams. Referrals are made to doctors willing to perform abortions despite their illegality because of medieval, menopausal politicians. Call them for an appointment before you go out there. They are about to establish an office on the Lower East Side.

FREE INFORMATION — Yippie: Youth International Party, 32 Union Square East, 982-5090.
ESSO — East Side Service Organization, 341 East 10th St., 533-5930.

DIAL-A-DEMONSTRATION — 924-6315 to find out about antiwar rallies and demonstrations.

DIAL-A-SATELLITE — TR 3-0404 to find out schedules of satellites.

★ ★ ★

NERVOUS can be dialed for the time.
WEATHER REPORT — WE 6-1212.
DIAL-A-PRAYER — CI 6-4200. God is a long-distance call.

★ ★ ★

If you want someone to talk you out of jumping out of a window call IN 2-3322.

★ ★ ★

If you have nothing to do for a few minutes, call the Pentagon (collect) and ask for Colonel John Masters of the Inter-Communication Center. Ask him how the war's going. (202) LI 5-6700.

★ ★ ★

If you want the latest news information you can call the wire services: **AP** is PL 7-1312 or **UPI** is MU 2-0400.

LIBERATION NEWS SERVICE — At 3064 Broadway and 121st Street will give you up to the minute coverage of movement news both national and local, as well as a more accurate picture of what's going on. Call 865-1360. By the way, what is going on?

THE EAST VILLAGE OTHER — Office at 105 Second Avenue and 6th Street, 228-8640 might be able to answer some of your questions.

THE DAILY NEWS INFORMATION BUREAU — 220 East 42nd Street, MU 2-1234, will try to answer any question you put to them unless it's "Why do we need the Daily News?"

THE NEW YORK TIMES RESEARCH BUREAU — 229 West 43rd Street, LA 4-1000 will research news questions that pertain to the past three months if you believe there was a past three months.

★ ★ ★

FREE lessons in a variety of skills such as plumbing, electricity, jewelry making, construction and woodworking are provided by the Mechanics Institute, 20 West 44th Street. Call or write them well in advance for a schedule. You must sign up early for lessons as they try to maintain small courses. MU 7-4279.

★ ★ ★

Ron Rosen at 68 Thompson Street will give you free Karate lessons if he considers you in the movement.

★ ★ ★

FREE YOGA LESSONS — Yoga Institute, 50 East 81st Street, LE 5-0126. Call in advance for lecture schedule. You might be asked to do some voluntary kitchen yoga after the lessons.

★ ★ ★

FREE RENT — There are many abandoned buildings that are still habitable, especially if you know someone with electrical skills who, with a minimum of effort can supply you with free electricity. You can be busted for criminal trespassing but many people are getting away with it. If you are already in an apartment, eviction proceedings in New York take about six months even if you don't pay rent.

You can sleep in the parks during the day. Day or night you can sleep on the roofs which are fairly safe and comfortable if you can find a shady spot. The tar gets very hot when the sun comes out. Make friends with someone in the building, then if the cops or landlord or other residents give you a problem you can say you are staying with someone in the building. Stay out of hallways, don't sleep on streets or stoops, or in the parks at night.

★ ★ ★

FREE BEACHES — Coney Island Beach (ES 2-1670) and Manhattan Beach on Oriental Boulevard (DE 2-6794) are two in Brooklyn that are free. Call for directions on how to get there. The Bronx offers Orchard Beach, call TT 5-1828 for information.

★ ★ ★

FREE COLLEGE — If you want to go to college free send away for the schedule of courses at the college of your choice. Pick your courses and walk into the designated classrooms. In some smaller classes this might be a problem but in large classes, of which there are hundreds in New York, there is no problem. If you need books for the course, write to the publisher telling him you are a lecturer at some school and are considering using the book in your course.

★ ★ ★

FREE THEATRE — The Dramatic Worshop — Studio # 808, Carnegie Hall Building, 881 Seventh Avenue at 56th Street. Free on Friday, Saturday and Sunday at 8:15 P.M., JU 6-4800 for information.

New York Shakespeare Festival — Delacourte Theatre, Central Park. Every night except Monday. Performance begins at 8:00 P.M. but get there before 6:00 P.M. to be assured tickets.

Pageant Players, The 6th Street Theatre Group and other street theatre groups perform on various street corners, particularly on the Lower East Side. Free Theatre is also provided at the **United Nations** building and the **Stock Exchange** on Wall Street, if you enjoy seventeenth century comedy.

★ ★ ★

If you look relatively straight you can sneak into conventions and get all kinds of free drinks, snacks and samples. Call the **New York Convention Bureau**, 90 East 42nd Street, MU 7-1300 for information. You can also get free tickets to theatre events here at 9:00 A.M.

★ ★ ★

FREE MOVIES — **New York Historical Society** — Central Park West and 77th Street. Hollywood movies every Saturday afternoon. Call TR 3-3400 for schedule.

Metropolitan Museum of Art — Fifth Avenue and 82nd Street. Art films Mondays at 3:00 P.M. Call TR 9-5500 for schedule.

New York University — Has a very good free movie program as well as poetry, lectures, and theatre presentations. Call the Program Director's Office, 598-2026 for schedule.

Millenium Film Workshop — 2 East 2nd Street. Fridays beginning at 7:15 P.M. open screening of films by underground directors.

★ ★ ★

This is our favorite way to sneak into a regular movie theatre: Arrive just as the show is emptying out and join the line leaving the theatre. Exclaiming, "Oh, my gosh!" slap your forehead, turn around and return, telling the usher you left your hat, pocketbook, etc., inside. Once you're in the theatre just take a seat and wait for the next show. Another method is to call the theatre early and pose as a film critic for one of the mini magazines and ask to be placed on the "O. K. list." Usually this works.

This works very well at pre-released screenings. You can phone the various screening studios and find out what they are screening.

★ ★ ★

FREE MUSIC — **Greenwich House of Music School** — 46 Barrow Street (of Seventh Avenue), West Village. Fridays at 8:30 P.M. Classical.
Donnell Library Center — 20 West 53rd Street. Schedule found in "Calendar of Events" at any library. Classical.

Frick Museum — 1 East 70th Street. BU 8-0700. Concerts every Sunday afternoon. The best of the classical offerings. You must do some red tape work though. Send self - addressed stamped envelope that will arrive on Monday before the date you wish to go. One letter — one ticket.

The Group Image — Performs every Wednesday night at the Hotel Diplomat on West 43rd Street between Sixth and Seventh Avenues, and you can get in free if you say you have no money (sometimes). If you promise to take your clothes off it's definitely free. If you ball on the dance floor, you get a season's pass.

Filmore East — 105 Second Avenue. If you live in the Lower East Side you can generally get into the Fillmore East after the show has started, if there are seats. Just go up to the door with a half way decent story. You're with the diggers or Evo or something will generally work.

★ ★ ★

There are various free festivals put on in Central Park. You can call the **City Parks Departments** for a schedule at 734-1000.

Washington Square in the West Village is always jumping on Sunday. Check out the Banana Singers either here or on St. Mark's Place. Cop a kazoo in Woolworths or a tambourine and join the band.

★ ★ ★

FREE MUSEUMS — **Metropolitan Museum** — Fifth Avenue and 82nd Street.

Frick Museum — 1 East 70th Street. Great when you're stoned. Closed Mondays.

The Cloisters — Weekdays 10 A.M. to 5 P.M., Sundays 1 P.M. to 6 P.M. Take IND Eighth Avenue express (A train) to 190th Street station and walk a few blocks. The #4 Fifth Avenue bus also goes all the way up and it's a pleasant ride. One of the best trip places in town in medieval setting.

Brooklyn Museum — Eastern Parkway and Washington Avenue. Egyptian stuff best in the world outside of Egypt. Take IRT (Broadway Line) express train to Brooklyn Museum station.

Museum of the American Indian — Broadway at 155th Street. The largest Indian museum in the world. Open Tuesday to Sunday 1 to 5 P.M. Take IRT (Broadway Line) local to 157th Street station.

Museum of Natural History — Central Park West and 79th Street. Great dinosaurs and other stuff. Weekdays 10 - 5 P.M., Sunday 1 - 5 P.M.

The Hispanic Society of America — Broadway between 15th and 156th Streets. The best Spanish art collection in the city.

Asia House Gallery — 112 East 64th Street. Art objects from the Far East.

Marine Museum of the Seaman's Church — 25 South Street. All kinds of model ships and sea stuff.

Chase Manhattan Bank Museum of Money — 1256 Sixth Avenue. Free people consider property as theft and regard all banks, especially Chase Manhattan ones, as museums.

★ ★ ★

THE STATEN ISLAND FERRY — Not free, but a nickel each way for a five mile ocean voyage around the southern tip of Manhattan is worth it. Take IRT (Broadway Line) to South Ferry, local only. Ferry leaves every half hour day and night.

★ ★ ★

FREE CRICKET MATCHES — At both Van Cortland Park in the Bronx and Walker Park on Staten Island every Sunday afternoon. Get schedule from British Travel Association, 43 West 61st Street. At Walker Park free tea and crumpets are served during intermission.

★ ★ ★

FREE POETRY, LECTURES, ETC. — The best advice here is to see the back page of the Village Voice for free events that week. There are a variety of talks given at the **Free School**, 20 East 14th Street. Call 675-7424 for information. For free brochures about free cultural events in New York go to **Cultural Information Center**, 148 West 57th Street.

★ ★ ★

FREE SWIMMING POOLS
1. — East 23rd Street and Asser Levy Place (near Avenue A). Indoor and outdoor pools, plus gymnasium.
2. — 83 Carmine Street (at Seventh Avenue, West Village). Indoor and outdoor pools plus gymnasium.
Bring your own swim suit and towel. 35c admission at certain times after 1:00 P.M. if you are over 14 years of age.

★ ★ ★

BRONX ZOO — Bronx and Pelham Parkways. Largest zoo in the U. S. Great collection of animals in natural settings. IRT Broadway (Dyre Avenue line) to 180th Street station and walk north. Free every day but Tuesday, Wednesday and Thursday when cost is 25c.
BOTANICAL GARDENS — 1000 Washington Avenue, Brooklyn. Another peaceful trip center. This and the Cloisters best in New York if you want to get away from it all quickly. Open 8:30 A.M. 'til dusk. Take IRT (Broadway line) to the Brooklyn Museum station.
FREE PARK EVENTS—All kinds of events in the Parks are free. Call 755-4100 for a recorded announcement of week's events.

★ ★ ★

You can get free posters, literature and books from the various missions to the United Nations located on the East Side near the U.N. building. The Cuban Mission, 6 E. 67th Street, will give you free copies of Granma, the Cuban newspaper, **Man and Socialism in Cuba**, a book by Che Guevara, and other literature. Ask for Mr. Jimenez.

You can get fingerprinted free and have your phone tapped at no expense by going to the F.B.I. at 201 East 69th Street. Call LE 5-7700, ask for J. Hoover. Tell him you're Walter Jenkins.

★ ★ ★

FREE PETS — ASPCA, 441 East 92nd Street and York Avenue. TR 6-7700. Dogs, cats, some birds and other pets. Tell them you're from out of town if you want a dog and you will not have to pay the $5.00 license fee. Have them inspect and innoculate the pet, which they do free of charge.

★ ★ ★

DRAFT RESISTANCE ADVICE — Many of you have problems that require draft counseling or maybe you have gone AWOL and need advice. There are numerous groups that will help out. Go down to 5 Beekman Street (near City Hall) and find your way to the 10th floor. There are many anti-draft groups located there who will give you the right kind of information. Call the Resistance, 732-4272 for details.

★ ★ ★

FREE CLOTHING REPAIRS — All Wallach stores feature a service that includes sewing on buttons, free shoe horns, and shoe laces, mending pants pockets and linings, punches extra holes in belts, and a number of other free services.

★ ★ ★

FREE CARS — If you want to travel a long distance the auto transportation agencies are a great deal. Look in the Yellow Pages under Automobile Transportation and Trucking. You must be over 21 and have a valid driver's license. Call them up and tell them when and where you want to go and they will tell you if they have a car. They give you the car and a tank of gas free. You pay the rest. Go to pick up the car alone, then get some people who also want to go to help with expenses. You can make San Francisco for about $80.00 in tolls and gas in four days without pushing. Usually you have the car for longer and can make a whole thing out of it. You must look "straight" when you go to the agency.

★ ★ ★

If you would like to meet a real ghost, write Hans Holzer c/o New York Committee for Investigation of Paranormal Research, 140 Riverside Drive, New York, N. Y. He'll put you in touch for free.

★ ★ ★

RADIO FREE NEW YORK — WBAI-FM, 99.5 on your dial, 30 East 39th Street, OX 7-2288, after midnight radio station provides air time for free souls who need help or offer it.

★ ★ ★

NEW YORK SCENES, a magazine, has a monthly column called "The Free Loader" with good advice on getting stuff free.

★ ★ ★

MIMEOGRAPH MACHINE — Both the ESSO office and Yippie have a free mimeo machine that you can use to print poetry, criticism, your life story or anything else.

★ ★ ★

FREE BAKERY — Every Wednesday some people get together and cook bread at St. Mark's Church on the Bowerie, Second Avenue and 10th Street.

★ ★ ★

Write to major corporations and tell them you bought one of their products and it doesn't work, or it shits, or it tastes bad. Most firms will send you up to a case of merchandise just to get you off their back. Try Tootsie Roll, Campbell's Soup and cigarette companies for starters. Also General Mills for cereals. Write to their public relations office. One day at the library and a few stamps will get you tons of stuff.

★ ★ ★

CLAP AND THE TASMANIAN PIG FEVER — Clap (syphilis and

gonorrhea) and Tasmanian Pig Fever (TPF) are two diseases you can easily pick up for free on the Lower East Side. One, the Clap, you catch, and the other, TPF, catches you. The Clap comes from balling. There are some that claim they get it from sitting on a toilet seat but that is possible only if you dig that position. Generally, using a prophylactic will prevent the spreading of Clap. If you don't use them and you ball a lot your chances of picking it up are pretty good. Syphilis usually begins with a sore which may look like a cold sore or any other kind of sore or pimple around your sex organ. Soon the sore disappears, even without treatment, and is often followed by an inflamation of the mouth and throat, and rashes on the body. These symptoms also disappear without any treatment. But even if these outer signs disappear the disease remains if untreated. If it remains untreated years later syphilis can cause serious trouble such as heart disease, blindness, insanity, and paralysis.

Gonorrhea is more common than syphilis. The first sign of gonorrhea is a discharge from your sex organ. It may not be noticed in women. In men there is usually itching and burning of the affected areas. If untreated it can result in permanent damage to sex glands. Both syphilis and gonorrhea can be cured in a short time with proper medical attention. The doctor's instructions must be followed to the letter if you want to shake the disease. Sometimes someone will get a shot of penicillin, go home and wait three days, and seeing no change in his condition he will assume the treatment is not working and not go back for more. Some strains are resistant to penicillin but will respond to other medication. Keep going to the clinic until the doctor says No. Free Treatment regardless of age is available for Lower East Side residents at the **Chelsea Hygiene Center,** 303 Ninth Avenue at 27th Street. Call LA 4-2537 for more free information. You can also gets tests for a variety of other illnesses here, including hepatitis, which is common and dangerous. Free cancer check-ups also given. Day and night phone information at 269-5300.

★ ★ ★

Tasmanian Pig Fever is a disease common to the Lower

East Side. It's the **cops**. You are liable to get busted for a variety of reasons. Let's face it, the Lower East Side is a ghetto and getting busted by a cop is common in any American ghetto. The following is some general basic advice and some help on the chief causes for busts — dope and runaways, although runaways are not technically busted.

The TPF is the riot control squad in New York and is called out to handle many street demonstrations. The local police come out of the Ninth Precinct located on 5th Street between First and Second Avenues. The local cops are under the direction of Lieutenant Joe Fink. There are numerous arrests down here and a working knowledge of what to do about the cops can be very helpful.

Never let cops in your house if they do not have a search warrant. Ask them to slip it under the door. They only have a right to enter without a search warrant if they have strong reason to believe a crime is being committed on the premises. Most cases without a search warrant are thrown out of court. If you are arrested, give your name and address. If you do not you will have bail trouble. You can give a friend's address. Do not discuss any details of your case with the police. Demand to see your lawyer (See Free Legal Aid Section). You are allowed a phone call and generally they will give you three. Call your closest friend and tell him you are arrested. He should be instructed to meet you in court at **100 Centre Street**. On the fourth floor your friend can find out what courtroom you will appear in for arraignment. There is a Legal Aid lawyer in the courtroom who will handle the arraignment. If the charges are misdemeanors he should be used; if the charges are felonies you might be advised to get help from a private lawyer, Mobilization for Youth or some other agency. A good lawyer can get a bail reduction that can save you a good deal of time if you are hard up for bread. Bail depends on a variety of factors ranging from previous arrests to the judge's hangover. It can be put up in collateral, i.e. a bank book, or often there is a cash alternative offered which amounts to about 10 to 20% of the bail. Try and have your friend show up with at least a hundred dollars in cash. For very high bail there are the bail bondsmen in the area of the courthouse who will cover the bail for a fee not to exceed 5%. You will need what they term a solid citizen to sign the bail papers and perhaps put up some collateral.

DOPE BUSTS — Possession of less than a quarter of an ounce of pot is considered a misdemeanor. The penalty can be up to one year. In actuality, a conviction for possession is very rare. The New York courts are quite lenient on this charge. More than a quarter of an ounce is considered possession with intent to sell. This along with sale (to an agent) are considered felonies and punishable by terms of up to 15 years in prison. A few precautions are in order. If you are carrying when busted eat it as soon as it is cool. Never sell to someone you do not know. Never make a sale with two other people present. Agents always buy with another person or agent present as a witness. Never sell to anyone facing an indictment for they are subject to pressure. Undercover agents have some pretty interesting disguises. Black undercover cops are very hard to spot. Often undercover cops wear beards and moustaches but few, contrary to rumor, have very long hair. Long hair that takes a year to grow is not possible since agents are switched around and anyway long hair doesn't grow in Queens. Undercover cops always carry a gun so look out for that noticeable bulge or a jacket being worn on a hot day.

There is a new bill already passed, waiting for the governor's signature, that would upgrade the dope penalties, for example, sale of pot to a minor could get you up to life imprisonment. If this bill is passed and you are caught selling to a minor, pull out a gun and shoot the kid. You can only get 10-20 years for first degree manslaughter and can be paroled in 6 years. Acid and other dope, although against the law rarely result in busts and even less in convictions (heroin is another thing, of course). There are too many technicalities involved in analyzing the substance, many such as STP are not covered by the law. For this reason, they generally go after the grass unless there is a major production or sale involved.

RUNAWAYS — Laws governing runaways are equally ridiculous. Persons who look underage (under 16 for males, under 18 for females) can be stopped by a cop anytime and asked to produce identification. If you are underage or do not have identification to prove otherwise you can be brought to the police station. There your parents or guardian is called. If you have permission to be here they let you go, if not, your parents can pick you up there. If they don't want you, you can be sent to the Youth Detention House which is a very bad trip indeed. If you are a runaway, get fake identification and quick. People who put up runaways are subject to arrest for contributing to the delinquency for a minor. If you want to go home and need a contact or if you want to stay a few days in a good place call **Judson Memorial Church** in Washington Square, GR 7-0351. This is the first year this program has been in effect but the people running it are cool. If you don't want them to call your parents or the cops they assure us they will not. They can house and feed about twenty-five young people.

★ ★ ★

DEMONSTRATIONS — A word should be said about demonstrations. Demonstrations with large numbers of arrests rarely result in convictions. Lawyers inform us of the over 3,000 arrests in recent anti-war, yippie demonstrations, etc. there have been no convictions. This does not mean things couldn't change drastically but these are the facts up to now.

★ ★ ★

Remember when arrested give only your name and address. Demand a search warrant if they want to come into your pad. The only know cure for Tasmanian Pig Fever is revolution. Paranoids unite!

★ ★ ★

DOPE — As you probably know, most dope is illegal, therefore some risks are always involved in buying and selling. In the legal section we have discussed the selling problems. Now let us consider the problems involved in buying. Arrests are not a problem unless you are inside and happen to get caught in a raid on a major dealer. What is a major hazard is getting burned. The usual trick is to take your dough and just vanish, leaving you standing on the street. Another method is substituting oregano or parsely for grass, chewing tobacco as hash, and aspirin and barbiturates as acid. A general rule is no bread up front. If you're getting an ounce or more of grass you are entitled to sample it. Hash can also be sampled. If you're considering buying a large amount of acid, buy one tab for a sample and try it first. Another rule is to buy from a known dealer or a close friend.

Have you considered growing your own? Being a weed, grass is very easy to grow if it gets enough water and sun. Get your seeds together, travel over to Jersey or Staten Island, find a field and plant your seeds. Draw a furrow in the ground about half an inch deep and plant the seeds about two inches apart. Cover the seeds with soil and water the area. Returning every two weeks to tend your crop will be sufficient. No matter how high the shoots get they are smokeable if dried out but it is best to let them grow to maturity (when the flowers bloom). This takes three to four months depending on soil conditions and sunlight. With a little effort, you can grow kilos galore. Growing grass indoors is a big hassle but it can be done if you construct a planting box with a light bulb or artificial growing lamp. Some hardy souls have planted grass in Carl Schurz Park next to Gracie Mansion, 89th Street and East River Drive.

There are also legal highs, the most famous of which is bananas. Scrap the insides of the banana peel and roast in a 200° oven for a half hour or until dark brown. Crumble the scrapings and roll in a joint or pack in a pipe. This will produce a mild pot high.

Mornings glory seeds will produce a high similar to LSD if prepared properly. Use only the white, blue, or blue-white varieties that are not coated with chemicals. If they have been coated a good washing in alcohol will remove it. You need about 400 seeds to get you up there. Generally there are about 40 to 60 in a packet. We prefer the following method: grind the seeds in a pepper mill and stuff them into gelatin capsules that you can get in any drug store. Another method is to boil the seeds, strain the mixture and drink the liquid. It tastes bitter but it's easier than the grinding method. It's an 8-10 hour trip.

Whipped cream containers are 80% nitrous oxide or laughing gas. Hold the container upright and release the nozzle slowly as you inhale. It's really a gas; even the whipped cream gets you high.

Some people claim you can get high on cabbage centers. Others claim cigarette tobacco mixed with powdered aspirins will do the trick. A hint on grass: boil the twigs and seeds and make a very groovy tea — sort of a tea-tea.

★ ★ ★

BAD TRIPS — The best method for bringing a person down from a bad trip is calm, understanding talk by a sympathetic soul. Generally this works. Orange juice and sugar works well. A cup of sugar to a quart of orange juice. Drink as much as you can. **Niacinimide**, a vitamin B derivative also works. You need 1000 milligrams for every 100 micrograms of LSD. Say the tablets you have are 100 mg. That means ten tablets for each 100 micrograms of LSD. If you do not know the LSD dosage, assume 500 micrograms and use 50 tablets of Niacinimide. Too much Niacinimide cannot hurt you. Landing time for both the orange juice-sugar method and Niacinimide is between 30-40 minutes. Niacinimide has better results. It is available without a prescription and is fairly cheap. You can get a thousand tablets for about three dollars.

As a last resort you should call in a physician who can administer a tranquilizer, generally thorazine. Bellevue should be considered a bad trip.

Be careful of drugs you know nothing about. STP is only for people who have been into acid for a time. Heroin is addictive and can be a mighty expensive habit. Amphetamine, usually called A or meth or speed, is also quite dangerous if you don't know what you are doing. Both heroin and meth are self-destructive. They ruin your appetite, often causing malnutrition. Since they are needle drugs there is always the chance of missing a vein, which leads to a stiff arm for a few days or of contracting serum hepatitis from unsterilized needles. You can kick the habit by just refusing to take it for a few weeks or switching to a groovier drug. Don't get hooked on any drug, whether it be heroin, school, coca-cola, benzedrine, suburbia, meth, or politics. They can all rot your brain . . . Be advised.

COMMUNES — Communes can be a cheap and enjoyable way to live. They are a good tribal way to live in the city. Because they are tribes each has a personality of its own. This personality depends on the people in the commune and how well they get along together. For this reason the most important part of setting up a commune is choosing people who are compatible. It is vital that no member of the commune has any strong objection to any other member. More communes have been destroyed by incompatibility than any other single reason. People of similar interests (speed freaks with speed freaks, painters with painters, and revolutionaries with revolutionaries) should get together. Preferably the members of the commune should know each other before they begin setting up quarters.

Once there is a nucleus of 4 to 7 people that are compatible establishing a commune is not difficult. The first thing to do is rent an apartment. The initial cost will probably be two months rent. Don't pay more. The landlord is not legally allowed to ask for more than one month's rent as security. Don't go to a rental agency unless you are willing to pay an extra month's rent as a fee. Two ways you can find an apartment if you don't know of one are: walk up and down every street and look for rent signs; the other is to look inside the front doors of some buildings in the area for a sign giving the landlord's name. When you find buildings owned by one company there is a pretty good chance that the company owns other buildings in the area. Call that company and ask if they have any vacant apartments.

When you get an apartment, furnishing will be the next step. You can double your sleeping space by building loft or bunk beds. Nail two by fours securely from ceiling to floor about three feet from the walls where beds are wanted. Then build a frame out of two by fours at the height you want the beds. Make sure it is strong enough to hold the weight of people sleeping on it. Then nail a sheet of 3/4 inch plywood on the frame. Mattresses and other furniture can be gotten for free. See the section on free furniture. You can cop silverware in self-service restaurants.

How you govern your commune depends on where the member's heads are. One method which works well is the Indian tribal council in which from time to time all members of the tribe (commune) get together and discuss problems that come up and solutions are worked out. At the meeting it should be decided which members are responsible for the things that have to be done (i.e. cooking cleaning, raising the rent); this assures that they will be done. It is a good idea to have a meeting when you first form to make decisions on some of the important things that are sure to arise. The first is whether you want a crash pad or a commune. The difference is that a commune is a closed unit. Other people may join, but unlike a crash pad, they may not join for one day. Other things to consider are drugs (no drugs in the pad, communal stash, etc.), property (personal, communal), age limits and so on. The important thing to remember is that with experience and basic trust for each other, this form of tribal living is by far the best way to live in the city jungle. Ask around for an experienced commune and get one of their members to come to your first tribal meeting. The more stable communes that are established the sooner we can begin to realize a freer more humanistic society.

★ ★ ★

Revolution is Free. Venceremos!

★ ★ ★

"America is the land of the Free.

My ol' man George always told me that

Free means you don't pay."

Jim Metesky

www.ingramcontent.com/pod-product-compliance
Lightning Source LLC
Chambersburg PA
CBHW071942020426
42331CB00010B/2977